21st Century
Basic Skills
Library

KIDS CAN KEEP AIR CLEAN

by Cecilia Minden, PhD

Cherry Lake Publishing • Ann Arbor, Michigan

3

CHERRY LAKE
Publishing

Published in the United States of America
by Cherry Lake Publishing
Ann Arbor, Michigan
www.cherrylakepublishing.com

Photo Credits: Cover and page 1, ©Monkey Business Images/
Shutterstock, Inc.; page 4, ©highviews/Shutterstock, Inc., page 6,
©Sebastian Kaulitzki/Shutterstock, Inc.; page 8, ©Eric Isselée/
Shutterstock, Inc.; page 10, ©iStockphoto.com/caracterdesign; page 12,
©iStockphoto.com/bonniej; page 14, ©Johan Swanepoel/Shutterstock,
Inc.; page 16, ©Chris Twine/Shutterstock, Inc.; page 18, ©Morgan Lane
Photography/Shutterstock, Inc.; page 20, ©Kurhan/Shutterstock, Inc.

Library of Congress Cataloging-in-Publication Data
Minden, Cecilia.
  Kids can keep air clean/by Cecilia Minden.
      p. cm.—(Kids can go green!)
  Includes index.
  ISBN-13: 978-1-60279-871-7 (lib. bdg.)
  ISBN-10: 1-60279-871-0 (lib. bdg.)
  1. Air—Pollution—Juvenile literature. 2. Air quality—Juvenile literature.
3. Air quality management—Juvenile literature. I. Title.
  TD883.13.M56 2011
  363.739'2—dc22   2009049742

JNF
363.7392
MINDEN

Cherry Lake Publishing would like to acknowledge
the work of The Partnership for 21st Century Skills.
Please visit www.21stcenturyskills.org for more information.

Printed in the United States of America
Corporate Graphics Inc.
July 2010
CLFA07

TABLE OF CONTENTS

What Is in Our Air?

When you think of **layers**, you might think of a cake.

One cake is layered on top of another. Yum!

The air around Earth has **ozone** in some of its layers.

Ozone up high is good.

It **protects** us from the sun.

Why Should Air Be Clean?

Ozone down low is bad. It holds dirty air close to the ground.

Sometimes we can even see dirty air. It is called **smog**.

We **breathe** air closest to the ground.

Dirty air can make us sick.

Animals and plants are also hurt by dirty air.

11

How Can Kids Keep Air Clean?

You can start by walking more.

Most cars put harmful gases into the air.

When we use our cars less, we put less bad gas into the air.

Get an adult to help you read **labels**.

Some paints and cleaners can hurt the air we breathe.

We use **energy** to run things in our homes. Always turn off what you are not using.

Using less energy helps keep air clean.

Another way to use less energy is to **recycle**.

Help your family set up a recycling center in your home.

Clean air is important for all of us.

What will you do today to keep our air clean?

Find Out More

BOOK

Knight, M.J. *Why Should I Walk More Often?* Mankato, MN: Smart Apple Media, 2009.

WEB SITE

US EPA—We Can Make a Difference!
www.epa.gov/climatechange/kids/difference.html
Play games to learn more about keeping air clean.

Glossary

breathe (BREETH) to take air into and out of your lungs

energy (EN-ur-jee) power from coal, electricity, or other sources that makes machines work

labels (LAY-buhls) words on a paper attached to a product

layers (LAY-urz) thicknesses of something

ozone (OH-zohn) a kind of gas that is found in Earth's atmosphere

protects (pruh-TEKTS) guards from harm or damage

recycle (ree-SYE-kuhl) to process old items so they can be used to make new things

smog (SMOG) a mix of fog and smoke in the air

Home and School Connection

Use this list of words from the book to help your child become a better reader. Word games and writing activities can help beginning readers reinforce literacy skills.

a	cars	ground	labels	put	top
adult	center	harmful	layered	read	turn
air	clean	has	layers	recycle	up
all	cleaners	help	less	recycling	us
also	close	helps	low	run	use
always	closest	high	make	see	using
an	dirty	holds	might	set	walking
and	do	home	more	should	way
animals	down	homes	most	sick	we
another	Earth	how	not	smog	what
are	energy	hurt	of	some	when
around	even	important	off	sometimes	why
bad	family	in	on	start	will
be	for	into	one	sun	you
breathe	from	is	our	the	your
by	gas	it	ozone	things	yum
cake	gases	its	paints	think	
called	get	keep	plants	to	
can	good	kids	protects	today	

Index

About the Author

Cecilia Minden is the former Director of the Language and Literacy Program at the Harvard Graduate School of Education. She currently works as a literacy consultant for school and library publishers and is the author of more than 100 books for children.